£6.99

WELCOME

To the home of MYSTERY, INC.

ZOINKS!

Welcome to the Scooby-Doo Annual 2007! If you are Scooby's number 1 fan, this is the place to be. Join the Mystery, Inc. gang as they solve lots of spine-tingling, monster-packed mysteries. There are loads of crazy puzzles, fun games and ace activities for you to enjoy. Plus Scooby and the crew show you how to make your own fantastic craft projects. Like, how cool is that, man?

Get ready to join the gang for plenty of mysteries, monsters and more than a few Scooby Snacks!

SCOOBY-DOO AND THE SKELETON SKARE!

SCOOBY STORY

WELL, GANG, HERE WE ARE--THE SITE OF THE *YUKON WINTERSPORTS CHAMPION-SHIP!*

I DON'T GIVE A BONGO WHERE WE ARE, FREDDIE, AS LONG AS IT'S NOT, LIKE, THE *FARM OF FEAR!*

THE SITE OF OUR LAST CASE, SHAGGY? WHY?

TERRANCE GRIEP JR. --writer * JOE STATON --penciller
JEFF ALBRECHT--inker * TOM ORZECHOWSKI--letterer
PAUL BECTON --colorist * DIGITAL CHAMELEON--separations
HARVEY RICHARDS -- ass't editor * JOAN HILTY--editor

'CAUSE THAT *PHANTOM SCARECROW* WAS, LIKE, THE S-SP-SPOOKIEST MONSTER I EVER SAW...AND *THAT'S* SAYING SOMETHING!

WELL, SHAG, UNLESS YOU'RE AFRAID OF *CROWDS,* YOU SHOULD BE FINE. AND BESIDES, YOU SAY THAT AFTER *EVERY* CASE!

I WONDER WHERE TED IS! HE SAID THAT HE'D MEET US, UH...

...HERE...

TED! TED St. MORITZ! IT'S *YOU*!

I DIDN'T RECOGNIZE YOU IN THAT OUTFIT! I'LL BET YOUR OWN *MOTHER* WOULDN'T!

HEY, GUYS! HAVE YOU BEEN HERE LONG?

ACTUALLY, TED, WE JUST GOT HERE. WE HAVEN'T HAD A CHANCE TO LOOK AROUND.

WELL, THEN... LET ME SHOW YOU ON MY WAY TO THE TRACK!

SEE, EACH COMPETITOR--OR *SLIDER*--IN MY EVENT GETS TO MAKE FOUR RUNS FROM START TO FINISH, AND KEEPS HIS *BEST* TIME. SO FAR, I'M IN THE LEAD...

...KNOCK ON WOOD!

THIS PROPERTY IS SO *BEAUTIFUL*, TED...AND WHAT A *BIG CROWD*!

NK NK

YEAH. THE ONLY PEOPLE NOT WATCHING THE *SKELETON CHAMPIONSHIP* ARE THE OCCUPANTS OF THE LOCAL *PRISON*!

"S-SK-SKELETON"?

OH, "SKELETON" JUST REFERS TO THE CHASSIS OF THE ORIGINAL SLEDS, WHICH RESEMBLED A SET OF *BONES*.

RONES...?

"THAT'S LARRY "HARD LUCK" HARDWICK, OUR *SLOWEST* RIDER, MAKING HIS FINAL RUN!"

"I'VE GOT TO GET FASTBONE ACROSS THE FINISH LINE... OR *FLEA* WILL WIN THE CHAMPIONSHIP!"

WELL, WHAT ABOUT A *SUBSTITUTE*? I COULD...

FRED, ARE YOU PULLING MY LEG? WITH YOUR WIDE SHOULDERS, I DON'T THINK YOU'D FIT DOWN THE CHUTE. AND YOU'RE TOO HEAVY!

A SUBSTITUTE WOULD HAVE TO BE LIGHTER. SOMEONE LIKE...

SOMEONE LIKE WHO?

OH, SHAAAAA-GGEEEEE--!

WE'VE GOT A GHOST TO GRAB AND A RACE TO RUN. HERE'S MY *PLAN*...

LIKE, HERE WE GO AGAIN...

SCOOBY

⑩

CONTINUED ON PAGE 14

Join the gang!

Join Mystery, Inc. for a day as they battle bad guys and solve mysteries. Play the game with a friend – all you need is a dice and some counters.

THE MYSTERY MACHINE

HOP IN THE MYSTERY MACHINE AND LET'S GO!

1 Stop to grab some bagels for breakfast. Miss a turn.

2

3 The Mystery Machine gets a flat tyre. Miss a turn to repair it.

6 Fred gets a call, there's a spook on the loose! Run to space 8 and catch it.

5

4

7

You help Velma to spot some clues. Go forward one space.

8

9 Daphne falls through a trap door. Miss a turn and help her

10

the Malt Shop

13

Shaggy gets spooked by a vampire. Hide behind space 8.

12

11 The gang stop at The Malt Shop for lunch. Skip a turn.

You help the gang to solve the mystery of a mad mummy. Take another turn.

Throw an even number to finish and you'll be home in time for tea!

FINISH

14

THE SCOOBY CREW

Get to know Scooby and his supersleuth pals with these Mystery, Inc. case notes!

GROOVY SCOOBY

Scooby-Doo is a goofy Great Dane and he belongs to Shaggy.

Scooby's full name is Scoobert-Doo. He is famous for two things - his fear of all things spooky and his love of food!

Scooby | FAST FACTS

ADDRESS: A kennel in Shaggy's backyard

AGE: 7

OCCUPATION: Man's best friend (Daphne and Velma's too)

LIKES: Pizza with ice cream on top

DISLIKES: Anything that goes bump in the night

CASE NO. 49379

Danger Prone Daphne

Super-stylish Daphne Blake loves mystery-solving but often falls into traps, giving her the nickname Danger Prone Daphne.

Daphne's father is a millionaire and bought the Mystery Machine for the gang.

Daphne | FAST FACTS

ADDRESS: 9000 Easy Street, Coolsville

AGE: 16

OCCUPATION: Stylish supersleuth

LIKES: Shopping

DISLIKES: Getting trapped by Tar Monsters

CASE NO. 49374

Fearless Fred

Freddie Jones is the leader of Mystery, Inc.

Fred is confident, brave and never gets spooked by gurning ghouls. His hobbies include creating inventions and his ambition is to become a mystery writer.

Super-smart Velma

Velma may be the youngest member of the gang but she also has the best track record for solving mysteries!

Velma is a real brainbox and she dreams of becoming a research scientist for NASA when she is older.

Velma FAST FACTS

ADDRESS: 316 Circle Drive, Coolsville

AGE: 15

OCCUPATION: Brainbox detective

LIKES: Tracking down clues

DISLIKES: Wearing glasses because she is always losing them!

CASE NO. 49377

Fred FAST FACTS

ADDRESS: 123 Tuna Lane, Coolsville

AGE: 16

OCCUPATION: Leader of the pack

LIKES: Playing American Football

DISLIKES: Being beaten by a villain

CASE NO. 493

THE MYSTERY MACHINE

The gang wouldn't get very far without the Mystery Machine!

It is equipped with a built-in monster tracking radar, a computer, video monitors, a first aid kit, a photography dark room and a picnic hamper full of snacks!

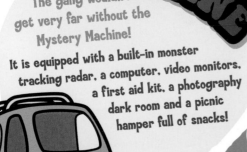

Scaredy Shaggy

Shaggy's real name is Norville Rogers.

You'll usually find Shaggy hanging out in the Malt Shop, enjoying a banana milkshake. He gets totally terrified when it comes to solving mysteries but he will tackle any ghost if there is a Scooby Snack on offer!

Shaggy FAST FACTS

ADDRESS: 224 Maple Street, Coolsville

AGE: 17

OCCUPATION: Hungry teenager

LIKES: Finding a box of Scooby Snacks

DISLIKES: Monsters, spiders and anything that makes you jump!

CASE NO. 49373

CONTINUED FROM PAGE 10

TRISTON SMITH!

RIGHT ON! TRISTON ASSUMED THE ROLE OF GHOST, KNOWING HE'D SCARE EACH SLIDER INTO CRASHING. THAT WAY, NO ONE WOULD NOTICE THAT THE JUDGE WAS MISSING. THEN...

WAIT A MINUTE, WAIT A MINUTE...

THIS DOESN'T MAKE ANY SENSE! BY HAUNTING THE TRACK, TRISTON SMITH WOULD ONLY RUIN HIS OWN RACE!

MAYBE. BUT HE'D MORE THAN MAKE UP THE DIFFERENCE BY *SMUGGLING INMATES* OUT OF THE LOCAL PRISON!

WHAAT? H-HOW...?

WHEN WE FIRST ARRIVED, WE DIDN'T RECOGNIZE TED BECAUSE OF HIS *OUTFIT*. THAT TURNED OUT TO BE OUR *FIRST* CLUE... EVEN BEFORE WE REALIZED WE'D STUMBLED UPON A MYSTERY!

THROUGH A HIDDEN TUNNEL LEFT OVER FROM THE OLD TOUCHWOOD LUMBER CAMP, MR. SMITH WAS ABLE TO SNEAK INMATES FROM THE PRISON AND INTO THE FINISH STATION.

WELL, SO WHAT--? THE SECOND A PRISONER LEFT THE STATION, HE'D JUST BE *RECAPTURED*!

NOT IF HE WAS *DISGUISED*! EACH INMATE WOULD EMERGE FROM THE FINISH STATION DRESSED AS A *SLIDER*!

A SLIDER? BUT...

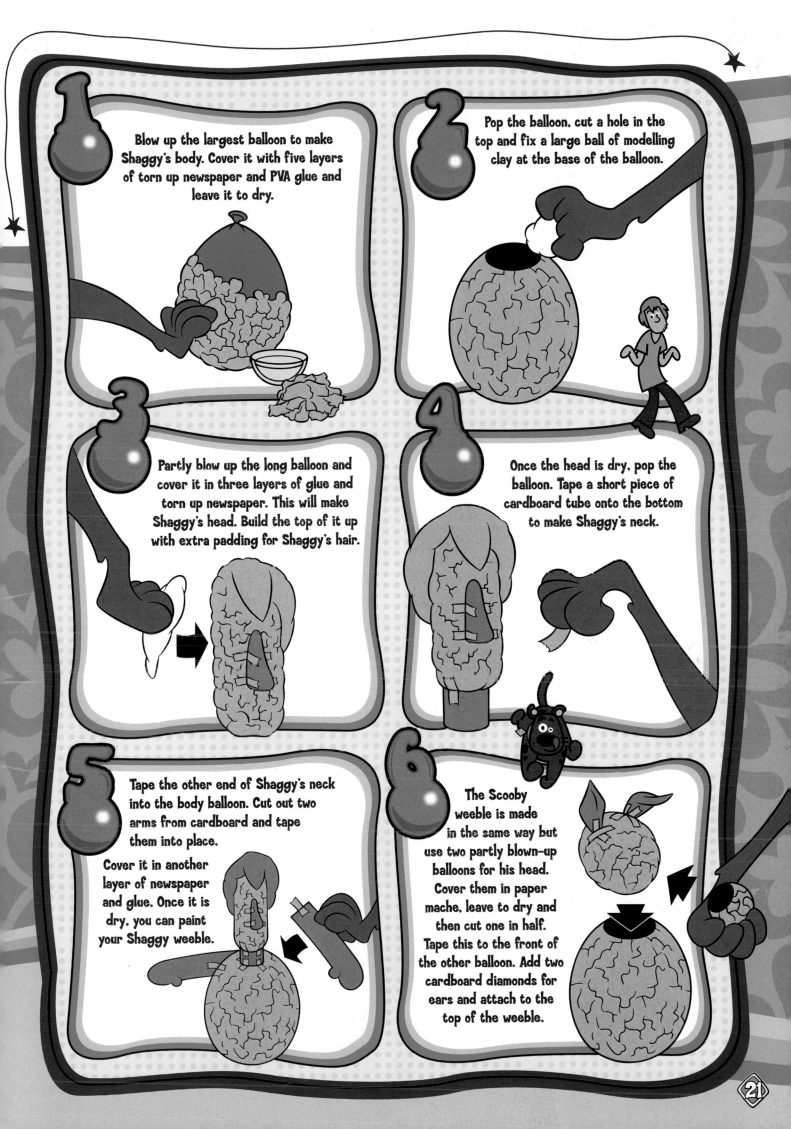

1. Blow up the largest balloon to make Shaggy's body. Cover it with five layers of torn up newspaper and PVA glue and leave it to dry.

2. Pop the balloon, cut a hole in the top and fix a large ball of modelling clay at the base of the balloon.

3. Partly blow up the long balloon and cover it in three layers of glue and torn up newspaper. This will make Shaggy's head. Build the top of it up with extra padding for Shaggy's hair.

4. Once the head is dry, pop the balloon. Tape a short piece of cardboard tube onto the bottom to make Shaggy's neck.

5. Tape the other end of Shaggy's neck into the body balloon. Cut out two arms from cardboard and tape them into place.

Cover it in another layer of newspaper and glue. Once it is dry, you can paint your Shaggy weeble.

6. The Scooby weeble is made in the same way but use two partly blown-up balloons for his head. Cover them in paper mache, leave to dry and then cut one in half. Tape this to the front of the other balloon. Add two cardboard diamonds for ears and attach to the top of the weeble.

THINGS THAT GO BUMP IN THE WALLS

JOHN ROZUM-Writer • PARIS CULLINS-Penciller
BOB PETRECCA-Inker
NICK J. NAP-Letterer • HEROIC AGE-Colorist
RACHEL GLUCKSTERN-Asst Editor
JOAN HILTY-Editor

THAT HOUSE BELONGED TO MY GRANDPARENTS, BUT NO ONE HAS LIVED IN IT FOR ALMOST FIFTEEN YEARS.

THAT'S WHY MY BROTHER AND I DECIDED TO HAVE IT TORN DOWN. THE PLACE IS SO ROTTED OUT, WE'RE BETTER OFF JUST SELLING THE LAND.

SWAK!

AS YOU CAN SEE, IT USED TO BE SUCH A BEAUTIFUL HOUSE, BUT AS THEY GOT OLDER, IT BECAME HARD FOR MY GRANDPARENTS TO KEEP IT UP.

IT'S ALREADY BEEN TWENTY YEARS SINCE MY GRANDPARENTS HAD A CREW WORKING ON AN ADDITION.

WOP!

THERE WAS SUPPOSED TO BE A DOOR AND A SCREENED-IN PORCH ADDED LATER, BUT A ROOM WAS AS FAR AS THEY GOT.

RFADY, SCOOB?

W

SWAK!

SO YOU DON'T REMEMBER ANY STRANGE PHENOMENA IN THAT HOUSE FROM WHEN YOU WERE A KID?

YOU MEAN GHOSTS? NO, AND MY FAMILY NEVER MENTIONED ANY, EITHER.

WHATEVER'S SCARING THOSE CONSTRUCTION WORKERS IS SOMETHING THAT MOVED IN AFTER MY GRANDPARENTS WERE GONE!

CONTINUED ON PAGE 28

THE HAUNTED GRAVEYARD

Have you got the sleuthing skills needed to be a top detective? Find out with this super-spooky game!

Study the scene below for one minute. Then cover it up and answer the questions about it on the opposite page. The aim of the game is to remember as much as you can about the scene so keep your eyes peeled!

QUESTION TIME!

Now it's time for the tricky bit! Have a go at answering these questions. Remember, dudes, taking a sneaky peek at the scene is soo not cool!

1 Where is the scene set?
a) in a graveyard b) in a museum
c) in a cafe

graveyard

2 What is Shaggy holding?
a) an ice cream b) a flower
c) a torch

a torch

3 Which of these three items doesn't appear in the scene?
a) 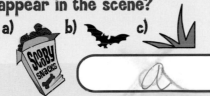 b) c)

a

4 There is a year written on one of the tombstones. Can you remember which year it is?
a) 1720 b) 1846 c) 1900

b

5 How many bats are there in the scene? a) 11 b) 2 c) 6

c

6 Who is standing behind Shaggy?
a) The Zombie b) Count Dracula
c) The Wicked Witch of the West

zombie

7 What is on Scooby's dog tag?
a) the letters SD b) a dog bone
c) Scooby-Doo

a

8 There is another spooky character in the scene. What is it?
a) a mummy b) a ghost c) a werewolf

a ghost

Answers: 1-A, 2-C, 3-A, 4-B, 5-C, 6-A, 7-A, 8-B.

SD mini toon

HMM. THIS ANCIENT MAP SAYS THERE SHOULD BE A TRAPDOOR AROUND HERE SOMEWHERE.

ER. GANG?

THAT'S OKAY, DAPHNE. WE'VE FOUND IT!

HE SAID *WE* WANTED TO SEE HIS BOSS, DONALD FRANK, *FAIL?*

THAT'S *EXACTLY* WHAT RANDY SAID.

WELL, DONALD'S A GOOD GUY, BUT BECAUSE HE HAD SOME *BAD LUCK* WITH A COUPLE OF RECENT JOBS, HE'S GOTTEN A LITTLE *PARANOID.*

SURE, WE'RE *RIVALS,* AND I WISH *MY* CONSTRUCTION COMPANY HAD GOTTEN THE JOB, BUT YOU CAN'T WIN 'EM ALL!

AFTER ALL, IT WAS *DON'S* DAD'S CREW THAT DID THE RENOVATIONS THERE 20 YEARS AGO, SO IT MAKES SENSE *DON* GOT THE JOB THIS TIME.

DON'S *DAD* WORKED ON THE HOUSE?

YEP, BUT ANYWAY, WITH THE MOLD MONSTER, I'M *GLAD* MY COMPANY DIDN'T GET THE JOB!

HOW DID YOU DO?

I THINK I'M SEEING SOME PIECES BEGINNING TO FIT.

I'LL CATCH UP WITH YOU AT THE HOUSE, BUT THERE ARE A FEW THINGS I WANT TO LOOK INTO FIRST.

IF I HAD KNOWN WE'D BE GOING TO THE CREEPY HOUSE, I'D HAVE STAYED WITH VELMA!

REE ROO!

COME ON, YOU-- LET'S GET THIS OVER WITH!

LOOK! THERE'S *SOMETHING* IN THAT BULLDOZER!

⊰PHEW⊱ IT'S JUST A BUNCHED-UP TARP. BUT SOMETHING'S *FREAKY* ABOUT THIS BULLDOZER!

LOOK! SOMEONE'S DEMOLISHED THE DASHBOARD. AND CHECK OUT THIS SLIME. *YEUUCH!!*

SKKRTT-CRUMP!

WHAT WAS THAT?

OUR CUE TO GET OUT OF HERE!

CLICK!

IT CAME FROM AROUND BACK, WHERE THE ADDITION WAS BUILT! LOOK-- FOOTPRINTS!

THE ADDITION IS THIS WAY...

THE NOISES HAVE STOPPED.

I HOPE THAT'S A *GOOD* THING!

WELL, THERE'S NO SIGN OF ANY MONSTER--BUT LOOK AT THIS *OPENED WALL.* I THOUGHT DONALD SAID THAT HE WASN'T ABLE TO START THE DEMOLITION.

BUT HERE ARE THE TOOLS THAT WERE USED...

...AND ONE HAS THE INITIALS "D.F." ENGRAVED ON THE *HANDLE!*

TWENTY YEARS AGO, WHEN THIS ADDITION WAS BUILT, THE INTENTION WAS TO ALSO ADD ON A SCREENED-IN PORCH, BUT THAT PORCH WAS NEVER BUILT.

THE REASON IS THAT WHEN THIS ADDITION WAS BEING BUILT, TWO *PAINTINGS* BELONGING TO THE OWNERS WERE STOLEN AND NEVER RECOVERED.

THE OWNERS SUSPECTED A MEMBER OF THE CONSTRUCTION CREW, *ENDING* THEIR RENOVATION PLANS!

THEY WERE *RIGHT.* DONALD FRANK STASHED THE PAINTINGS INSIDE THE WALL THAT WAS TO BE THE DOOR TO THE PORCH.

HE FIGURED HE'D BE ABLE TO RETRIEVE THEM WHEN THE PORCH WAS BUILT, BUT WHEN THOSE PLANS WERE CANCELED THE PAINTINGS LAY BEYOND HIS REACH...UNTIL NOW!

SHRRIIIIIPPP

THERE THEY ARE!

ALL HE HAD TO DO WAS GET THE PAINTINGS OUT, BUT HE COULDN'T BE DISCOVERED--HENCE THE *MOLD MONSTER DISGUISE.*

I'M TELLING YOU, I'VE BEEN *FRAMED!*

NOT AS NICELY FRAMED AS THESE PAINTINGS, THOUGH! NOW 'HOW 'BOUT THAT LUNCH PAIL?

ROOBY-ROOBY-ROO!

THE END

Doggie Doodle!

Follow these easy steps and create your own pictures of that super-scaredy Scooby-Doo!

1 Start by drawing a curved line in the centre and add three circles along it.

2 Draw lines for his arms and legs. Add triangles to the end of each line for a paw. Add a squiggly line for his tail.

3 Draw curved lines to join each of the three circles up. Add an oval for his nose. Use thin triangular shapes to build up his arms and legs.

4 Add some shape to his paws and draw in his collar. Rub out any lines that you no longer need.

5 Use the steps on the opposite page to draw his face. Draw in the spots on his coat and add his dog tag. When you are happy with your sketch, go over it with a fine black pen and rub out the pencil lines.

1

2

3

Start by drawing a sausage shape for Scooby's neck and an oval for his nose. Add his collar, tag and ears. Add the detail to his mouth and nose and sketch in two arch shapes for his eyes. Finally, add the details like his whiskers and eyebrows.

Now it's your turn! Have a go at adding your own Scooby sketch to the scene below.

ATLANTIC CITY! "AMERICA'S FAVORITE PLAYGROUND," WHERE PEOPLE COME FOR *GAMBLING, ENTERTAINMENT...*

WELCOME MISS TRI-STATE BEAUTY PAGEANT!

AWRIGHT, AWRIGHT! EVERYONE INTO LINE! LET'S GET THIS OVER WITH!

...AND *BEAUTY CONTESTS!*

ONE AT A TIME, PLEASE! FILL OUT YER *FORM--IN TRIPLICATE--* AN' TAKE YER *NUMBER.* AN' I'LL NEED *PHOTO I.D.*...!

GOSH! SO MUCH *PAPERWORK!*

TAKE YOUR TIME, DEAR-- DADDY WILL DROP YOUR BAGS IN THE *DRESSING ROOM.* Er...WHERE *IS* HER DRESSING ROOM EXACTLY?

BACKSTAGE, PAL! THERE'S ONLY *ONE,* SO EVERYBODY *SHARES.* NO *PRIMA DONNAS!*

GRACIOUS! WHEN'S THE LAST TIME THIS OLD PLACE WAS *CLEANED*--BEFORE OR AFTER *WORLD WAR II?*

cree-ee-eak...!

PLACE IS OVERRUN WITH MILDEW, DUST, COBWEBS AND HEAVEN KNOWS WHAT *ELSE...*

FRANK STROM -- Writer / **ANTHONY WILLIAMS** -- Penciller / **DAN DAVIS** -- Inker / **TOM ORZECHOWSKI** -- Letterer
PAUL BECTON -- Colorist / **SNO CONE** -- Separations / **HARVEY RICHARDS** -- Asst. Editor / **JOAN HILTY** -- Editor

SKREEE

POIT

...HUBBA-BUBBA-BUBBA...

...BUBBA-BUBBA-BUBBA...

RRAGGY?

...BUBBA-BUBBA-BUBBA...

SPLORSH!

LISTEN, FOLKS—LET'S ALL *STICK TOGETHER* SO WE CAN AVOID ANY PROBLEMS THAT...

FREDDIE, WE MAY ALREADY *HAVE* A PROBLEM. WHERE'S—?

DOES *THIS* BELONG TO *YOU?* FOUND IT IN TH' *WATER!*

SHAGGY!

CONTINUED ON PAGE 41

SHADOW SPOOKS!

These spooky shadows are making poor Scooby-Doo tremble with fear! Can you work out what each shadow belongs to?

Which two items don't have matching pairs?

ANSWERS: A-12, B-11, C-3, D-5, E-9, F-10, G-7, H-1, I-8, J-2
The two items without matching shadows are 4 and 6.

DAPHNE, WHAT--?

TH-TH-THERE REALLY *IS* A SIREN...≥SNIFF≤...JUST LIKE IN MYTHOLOGY...

...EXCEPT *THIS ONE'S* POWERS-- ≥KA-CHOO!≤-- ALSO WORK ON *WOMEN!*

WELL, *I'M* OUTTA HERE!

ME, TOO!

HEY! STOP! WE GOT A *PAGEANT* TO RUN HERE!

LET'S *GO,* GLORIA-- IF WE HURRY, WE CAN CATCH THE NEXT BUS FOR *PASSAIC!*

NO WAY, MARTY! I'M *STAYING!*

STAYING?!? GIRL, YOU HAVE LOST IT!

BUT I *HAVEN'T* LOST IT! IN FACT, I'M GONNA *WIN* THIS PAGEANT FOR SURE! IF THE *OTHER* CONTESTANTS QUIT, WHO'S LEFT TO CHALLENGE ME FOR THE CROWN?

ME. I'M OFFICIALLY ENTERING THE BEAUTY CONTEST!

groovyscopes

WITH THE MYSTERY, INC. GANG!

It's time to get mystic as the Scooby crew reveal what groovy things the stars have in store for you!

AQUARIUS (20 January-19 February)

Shaggy says: Like, stop right there you Aqua dudes! It's time to kick back and relax cos life is just one big roller coaster for you at the mo! But hey, I'd rather be on a roller coaster than a spooky ghost train! Those things make me shiver!

PISCES (20 February-20 March)

Daphne says: Jeepers! I hope you are feeling brave because there is something mysterious in the air! All will be revealed soon and one thing's for sure, it's gonna be really exciting!

ARIES (21 March-20 April)

Fred says: Well, guys, it's time for you to get organised! Things have been hectic lately but don't worry, a bit of planning and list-writing will get you back at the front of the race! Good luck!

TAURUS (21 April-21 May)

Velma says: The best way to solve a mystery is with team work so don't be afraid to ask for help. Who knows, your pals may be just as grateful if you put your brain cells together and get that problem solved!

GEMINI (22 May-22 June)

Shaggy says: Like, watch out cos things are about to get spooky-doo! Beware of cupboards and trapdoors cos these are fave hiding places for monsters. If you do bump into one, I suggest you turn and run as fast as you can. Or you can call Velma, she'll sort that silly spook out!

CANCER (23 June-23 July)

Daphne says: Lady Luck is your best gal pal at the moment and everything is going your way. Make the most of it and make sure you are wearing the must-have accessory of the season - a big smile!

LEO (24 July-23 August)

Fred says: Brave as a lion and ready for anything, that's you! You love an adventure and there are plenty coming your way. Don't forget to pack your tool kit and monster tracker as they are adventure essentials!

VIRGO (24 August-23 September)

Shaggy says: Like, d'ya know what I can see In your stars? A giant shopping bag! It's time to hit the shops! Treat yourself to a new game, book or pair of shoes, you totally deserve it! Have fun, dudes!

LIBRA (24 September-23 October)

Velma says: You have a big social event coming up and it is going to be so cool! So put those nerves to one side and get ready to have a totally top time!

SCORPIO (24 October-22 November)

Daphne says: School may not seem cool, but I reckon it rocks! Liven up your school week by starting a new lunchtime club for you and your pals. A Scooby club could be really cool!

SAGITTARIUS (23 November-22 December)

Shaggy says: Like, my crystal ball reckons it's time for you to grab a little "you time" and do the things that you enjoy most. So lemme see, that will be... pizza, snooze, snack... pizza, snooze, snack... perfect-o-tastic, dudes!

CAPRICORN (23 December-19 January)

Scooby says: Rit's rime for reating rots and rots of rooby racks! Save rome ror me! MM-mmmm! Buuuuurp! Ree-hee-he-hee!

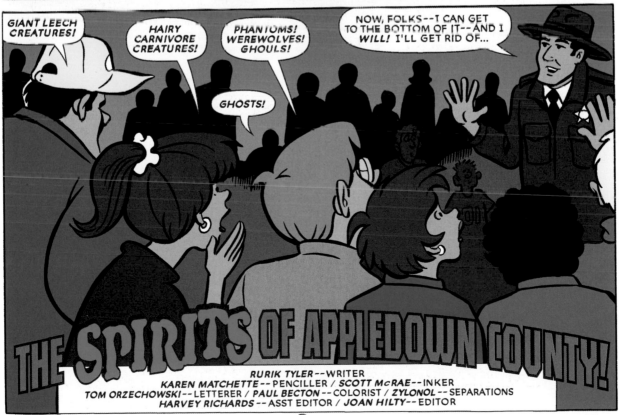

THE SPIRITS OF APPLEDOWN COUNTY!

RURIK TYLER -- WRITER
KAREN MATCHETTE -- PENCILLER / SCOTT McRAE -- INKER
TOM ORZECHOWSKI -- LETTERER / PAUL BECTON -- COLORIST / ZYLONOL -- SEPARATIONS
HARVEY RICHARDS -- ASST EDITOR / JOAN HILTY -- EDITOR

SOON...

I'M GLAD YOU YOUNGSTERS COULD COME. YOU'VE DEALT WITH WEIRD SIGHTINGS BEFORE?

YES WE HAVE...THOUGH KEEP IN MIND THAT AFTER YOU'VE SEEN SHAGGY HERE EAT A *BIRTHDAY CAKE SANDWICH,* NO SIGHTING SEEMS WEIRD.

SPEAKING OF BIRTHDAY CAKE SANDWICHES-- WHEN'S *LUNCH?*

SHERIFF, WHO WOULD HAVE SOMETHING TO *GAIN* FROM MONSTERS SCARING PEOPLE?

UM...

IN A LOT OF OUR CASES "GHOST SIGHTINGS" ARE USED TO BRING DOWN THE *VALUE* OF SOMETHING, SO THAT SOMEONE HAS AN EASIER TIME GETTING WHAT THEY WANT!

THAT DOESN'T FIT IN THIS CASE. THE GHOSTS ARE ALL OVER THE PLACE!

WELL, THIS IS A LITTLE HARD FOR ME TO SAY, BUT WHAT IF THE THING OF VALUE WAS A JOB-- *MY JOB?*

YOU THINK THE GHOSTS ARE TRYING TO MAKE YOU QUIT SO THAT THEY CAN TAKE OVER THE TOWN?

RIKES!

NO SON, I... LISTEN, THIS FELLOW *SINCLAIR* IS RUNNING AGAINST ME FOR SHERIFF. MAYBE *HE* SET IT ALL UP TO MAKE ME LOOK BAD!

RIGHT! IF THE SHERIFF CHASES THE GHOSTS, HE'LL LOOK FOOLISH--

--BUT IF HE IGNORES THE GHOSTS HE'LL LOOK LIKE HE IS NEGLECTING HIS DUTIES. MAYBE THE RIVAL *IS* RESPONSIBLE!

I DON'T KNOW, SINCLAIR IS FULL OF HOT AIR, BUT HE'S A GOOD PERSON... AT LEAST, I *THINK* HE IS!

CONTINUED ON PAGE 56

Head First!

Jinkies! A crazy monster bursting through your wall will add some Scooby style to your room! Follow these steps to make your own mad monster.

YOU WILL NEED

CARDBOARD, WHITE PAPER, SCISSORS, A LONG BALLOON, PVA GLUE, STICKY TAPE, NEWSPAPER, PAINTS AND A PAINTBRUSH.

1 Cut out a large oval of card. Spread a layer of glue around the outside edge. Tear up triangles of card and lay them around the oval, pointing inwards. Spread another layer of glue around the outside edge again. Tear up triangles of white paper and glue them on top of the card triangles.

2 Once it has dried, bend back the card and paper triangles from the centre of the oval. This will make it look as if there is a hole in the wall and the wallpaper is torn.

3 Partly blow up the balloon and cover it with three layers of torn up newspaper and PVA glue. Leave it to dry and pop the balloon.

4 Cut a slit into the balloon shape about two thirds of the way along it. Bend the balloon at this point and tape it at an angle, to form the monster's head and neck. Add cardboard eyes, triangles for spines and a long cardboard tongue.

5 Cover the monster with a layer of paper mache and leave it to dry. Tape the monster head onto the base board.

6 Paint the monster with bright colours and paint the base board behind the monster black. Once it is dry, you can fix your monster to your wall!

SCOOBY'S SNACK ATTACK!

Scooby-Doo is a real hungry hound!
Help him to track down all of these tasty
snacks hidden in the grid.

C	I	Y	O	M	E	L	E	T	T	E	S		
U	O	E	A	P	P	L	E	P	I	C		S
R	H	O	T	D	O	G	O	N	B	W		O
R	F	P	K	P	Y	I	M	E	S	O		O
Y	C	O	W	I	Q	P	I	C	B	E		B
W	E	P	H	Z	E	A	L	E	F	E		Y
A	A	S	O	Z	E	S	K	L	C	D		S
N	I	N	A	X	T	S	O	A	X	N		
R	A	D	P	E	J	A	H	L	K	S		A
E	N	C	H	I	P	S	A	L	E	L		C
J	A	P	A	B	C	S	K	Y	O	A		K
O	B	U	R	G	E	R	E	P	O	C		S

SCOOBY SNACKS   CAKE   PASTA   PIZZA

CURRY   OMELETTE   CHIPS   BANANA   BURGER

ICE LOLLY   HOT DOG   APPLE PIE   MILKSHAKE   COOKIES

Velma's Super Spooks!

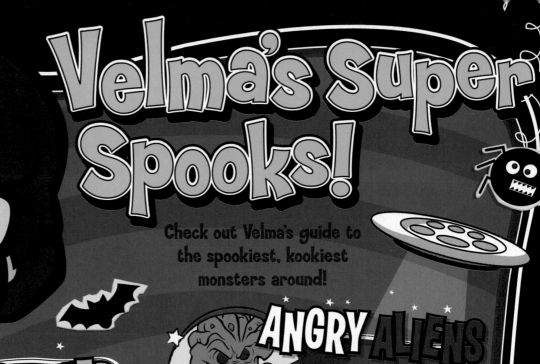

Check out Velma's guide to the spookiest, kookiest monsters around!

BIGFOOT BOTHER

Velma says: Bigfoot is one tough monster to tackle!

Bigfoot is said to live in the wilderness areas of Northern America. This large ape-like creature is covered in fur, has a large dome-shaped head and smells really bad! We have taken on several Bigfoot baddies in the past and they have all proved to be phoneys. However, I still reckon the real Bigfoot is out there somewhere!

MOUNTAINS

ANGRY ALIENS

Velma says: We have met lots of aliens in all shapes and sizes. Poor Scooby and Shaggy have even been taken on board an alien spacecraft, but luckily we managed to get them back!

Keep your eyes peeled for mysterious lights in the sky, circular markings in fields and boomerang shaped crafts whizzing through the sky. These have all been associated with alien activity. Give Mystery, Inc. a call if you spot anything spooky!

WEIRD WEREWOLF

Velma says: If there is a full moon and you hear a spooky howl, hide under your bed cos there's a werewolf on the loose!

These hairy howlers prowl around at the dead of night devouring anything that gets in their way. Then they return to their human form in the day and nobody knows their spooky secret! Mystery, Inc. have met a few werewolves. Luckily, they have all proved to be fakes in clever disguises!

RIP

MONSTER MASH

Unmuddle these letters to spell out Velma's favourite monster!

vparemi

vapmpiern

55

MONSTER *PAINTINGS!* A *WHISK BROOM* WITCH DOCTOR! A BONE-EATING OGRE *PUPPET!*

AND A *BOX PROJECTOR!* IT DISPLAYED *IMAGES* OF THOSE THINGS ALL OVER TOWN -- ON THE FOUNTAIN'S *MIST* AND OUR OWN DUSTY WINDSHIELD!

MR. PLATT, WHAT HAPPENED TO YOUR *BEARD?*

I...I HAD TO GLUE IT TO THIS FAKE HEAD!

AW, SHERIFF--WE WERE JUST *TELLING TALES* LIKE WE ALWAYS DO, WHEN THINGS GOT OUT OF HAND. WE THOUGHT IF WE COULD MAKE IT LOOK LIKE A *REAL* MYSTERY, WE WOULDN'T GET IN *TROUBLE!*

HA HA! THERE'S NO REAL HARM DONE--AND TELL YOU WHAT, MAYBE YOU COULD DISPLAY ALL THIS FANTASTIC ARTWORK AT THE *FALL PICNIC!*

BUT WE *DID* CALL *MYSTERY, INC.,* SO IF YOU TWO WOULD PAY THEM FOR THEIR TROUBLE...

IT'S A DEAL!

LIKE, WHEN THEY SEE HOW MUCH WE EAT AT THE PICNIC, THEY MIGHT WISH THERE *WAS* A FEE--IT WOULD BE *CHEAPER!*

THERE'S NO CHARGE, SHERIFF! INSTEAD, YOU COULD JUST INVITE US TO THE PICNIC!

SCANE'S FIX IT SHOP

DID YOU HEAR THAT? MY *PROJECTOR* WORKED SO WELL THAT I HAD THE ENTIRE *TOWN* SCARED!

WELL, MY *PAINTINGS* NOT ONLY SCARED THE TOWN, BUT THEY KEPT THE *COAST GUARD* FROM EVEN *SHOWING UP*...WHY, I HEARD ON THE *RADIO*...

THOSE TWO WILL *NEVER* LEARN!

HA HA HA HA HA

THE END!